IM
of A

SAN DIEGO S NAVAL
TRAINING CENTER

M000036517

IMAGES
of America

SAN DIEGO'S NAVAL
TRAINING CENTER

Jennifer A. Garey

ARCADIA
PUBLISHING

Published by Arcadia Publishing
Charleston SC, Chicago IL, Portsmouth NH, San Francisco CA

Printed in the United States of America

Library of Congress Catalog Card Number: 2008928799

For all general information contact Arcadia Publishing at:
Telephone 843-853-2070
Fax 843-853-0044
E-mail sales@arcadiapublishing.com
For customer service and orders:
Toll-Free 1-888-313-2665

Visit us on the Internet at www.arcadiapublishing.com

This book is dedicated to all the recruits, personnel, and officers of the Naval Training Center (NTC) San Diego and to all the new occupants of Liberty Station who continue to keep the NTC story alive.

CONTENTS

ACKNOWLEDGMENTS

So many deserve thanks for their ongoing task of preserving the history and spirit of NTC San Diego. The Corky McMillin Companies; C. W. Clark, Inc.; and the NTC Foundation together deserve special thanks for their monumental task of preserving and renovating the historic San Diego Naval Training Center into a thriving community at Liberty Station. Additional thanks go to the retailers and new occupants of Liberty Station, who by their participation either by organizing programming and displaying historic photographs and/or original artifact collections, help immensely in keeping the history and memory of NTC San Diego alive. Special thanks go to all of those who have allowed me to participate in keeping the history of NTC San Diego alive: first to Robert Witty, my good friend who has always believed in me and to whom I am forever grateful; Kim Elliott, an amazing woman whom I admire greatly and strive to emulate; Alan Ziter, a man with great vision and leadership to make the vision a reality; Marianne Gregson, a brilliant mind from whom I am learning every day; Cathy Sang, an amazing fund-raiser and a generous, considerate, wonderful friend; Stacy Goodman, a joy to work with and a woman with powerful inner strength; Greg Block, who made every project fun; Lew Witherspoon for explaining life in the U.S. Navy; and Clint Steed for providing hard-to-find information and for his never-ending quest to preserve NTC San Diego. Thank you Al Macias for everything you do to preserve the collections; thank you Rene Cornejo, Vickie S. Bell Cushing, and Rusty Burkett for loaning me your precious memories. Thanks to Richard Schleicher for sharing your knowledge and to Aaron C. Prah from the National Archives and Records Administration Pacific Region in Laguna Niguel (NARA) for locating and scanning photographs. Most importantly, thank you to Debbie Seracini for not giving up on me, to Scott Davis for calmly answering my questions again and again, and to all those at Acadia Publishing who actually made this possible. Their vision and efforts to preserve NTC San Diego will go far in keeping the memory alive.

All photographs, unless otherwise noted, are courtesy of the Department of the Navy, Naval Historical Center, and under the care of the Corky McMillin Companies.

INTRODUCTION

Since 1923, San Diego's Naval Training Center (NTC) has undergone many fluctuations in size and operations since its beginning as a Naval Training Station (NTS). NTC had a unique and symbiotic relationship with the city of San Diego with the additions of schools and later advanced schools. One of the unique attributes of San Diego's NTC was the Advance Training Programs and Diversity Programs, such as the Broadened Opportunity for Officer Selection Training (BOOST) and WAVES, Women Accepted for Volunteer Emergency Service. Many of the diversity programs and the advanced training programs such as television instruction began at San Diego's NTC. The high quality of training provided and the geographic location made San Diego's NTC the place where many wanted to train and many eventually retired. Numerous recruits, commanders, and civilians share fond memories of their time at NTC, and many became the men and women they are today because of the training and skills they learned while there.

The integral relationship between the U.S. Navy and San Diego began even before its inception, starting in 1916 with a dream of William Kettner, congressman from the 11th Congressional District of California and spokesperson for the San Diego Chamber of Commerce. The political elite of San Diego were looking at opportunities to put San Diego on the map. Competition was fierce with Los Angeles and San Francisco, both locations with ports and both soon to be the location of large railway hubs. San Diego, in response, wanted to be the first port of entry for the newly opened Panama Canal and was hopeful for a national rail line. These two options, if materialized, would bring in commerce and trade that would then build the community. They concocted the idea of having the 1915–1916 Panama-California Exposition to commemorate the opening of the Panama Canal, a grand public event to entice large corporations and political entities to fund the prospect and make San Diego the first port of entry. The main concern was the extensive marshland surrounding the proposed harbor. Although the exposition was a success, it did not bring in the backers the committee had hoped for. William Kettner had a different plan for the development of San Diego, one that he would continue to pursue relentlessly. He continued to court the U.S. Navy and its personnel in hopes of establishing a naval base in San Diego. Whether he envisioned the navy only dredging the harbor and creating one of the most beautiful and functional ports or whether he knew the navy would build the entire water infrastructure for the city of San Diego is not clear; however, once the navy came to San Diego, the benefits were evident. Funding for the acquisition of land and the deeds to much of the land itself came from San Diego local business, such as San Diego Securities, Union Trust and Company, and Southern Title Guaranty Company, among others. Navy dollars built the infrastructure and continued to rebuild and maintain it for 70 years. As NTC grew in size and numbers, the facility was reconfigured into numerous camps. Each camp was designated by location, and each camp was equipped with its own barracks, commissary, post office, medical facilities, mess hall, swimming pool, gym, and "grinder" (drill field). The camps were designated by names of regarded and decorated naval heroes, such as Camp John Paul Jones, Camp Lawrence, Camp Luce, Camp Decatur, Camp Farragut, and Camp Mahan. Over 70 years, NTC grew from an active training facility to a training center with the additions of schools and later advance schools. Much of the advanced school training and programs begun at NTC San Diego were found in no other naval training center. The BOOST program and the Radioman School, for example, were only located in NTC San Diego until the disestablishment.

NTC San Diego was the place where many men and women became a part of the community and part of world events. Much of our nation's critical moments were handled by men and women who trained at NTC San Diego. Many retired recruits and officers have returned to San Diego and continue to participate in the growth and memories of NTC by sharing their stories with the newly redeveloped NTC, now known as Liberty Station. These stories and memories are now in the care of the NTC Foundation and NTC Promenade, who is tasked with the mission to bring life back into the historic core of NTC.

The carefully thought-out restoration and reuse of the original buildings makes working in, living in, and visiting NTC San Diego/Liberty Station so unique. The thoughtful rehabilitation and reuse plans used by the Corky McMillin Companies and C. W. Clark, Inc., had never been undertaken by any other base renovation project in the nation. The development of a Historic Interpretive Master Plan for the Naval Training Center San Diego—developed and funded by the NTC Foundation, the Corky McMillin Companies, C. W. Clark, Inc., and the McCarthy Family Foundation—has set the standard for a legacy presence of the NTC story. Once again, NTC San Diego has become a model and a standard, first as a premier NTC and now as a model rehabilitation project. The history continues to be kept alive by businesses now occupying the original barracks, commissaries, and other NTC buildings, which communicate and educate all those who enter their establishments. NTC, once a thriving naval city full of learning and training, is now a thriving historic monument, with educational walking tours, retail, schools, churches, and cultural centers, as San Diego's NTC continues to be an integral part of the growth of San Diego.

Much of the source information for this book came from Mary E. Camacho, the NTC public affairs officer from 1995 to 1997, who showed great foresight in compiling material from the NTC newspaper, the *Hoist*, into a limited publication called *The Cradle of the Navy*. Additional resource materials include the Naval Historical Center, the U.S. Department of the Navy, the San Diego Historical Society, and the San Diego Navy Historical Association. Much information came through many discussions with recruits and officers who spent time at NTC San Diego.

THE SAILOR'S CREED

I am a United States Sailor.
I will support and defend the Constitution of the United States of America and I will obey the orders of those appointed over me.
I represent the fighting spirit of the Navy and those who have gone before me to defend freedom and democracy around the world.
I proudly serve my country's Navy combat team with Honor, Courage and Commitment.
I am committed to excellence and the fair treatment of all.

One

THE EARLY YEARS

This is an early view of the Naval Training Station (NTS). The tents of D Camp can be seen on the left above the circular boxing smoker, which is surrounded by marshland. Construction of the base occurred in phases; as the need for highly trained and specialized soldiers grew as a response to world events, the base grew along with the influx of recruits to accommodate those needs.

Sellers Plaza, seen from Lynton Road, is the oldest part of the historic Naval Training Station. The flagpole standing since the Naval Training Station's dedication can be seen just inside the famous Gate One. The anchor placed near this main entrance gate, the flag, and the gate itself are memorable features of Sellers Plaza. The plaza is named after the first base commander, Capt. Cmdr. David Foote Sellers.

Looking through Gate One from inside the Naval Training Station around the time of the commissioning, one sees many of the first-phase structures, which included a mess hall, a dispensary, fire house, pump house, headquarters building, four barracks, and Gate One. The commissioning ceremony took place within these gates in Sellers Plaza on June 1, 1923. The navy band performed while a mere 10 officers manned the station.

The dedication ceremony of the Naval Training Station took place on October 27, 1923, four months after it was commissioned. In this photograph, the flag is raised by Maxine Edmonds, a senior from San Diego High School. Capt. David Foote Sellers, the first commanding officer, was the host of the ceremony, and William Kettner had the honor of delivering the dedication speech. Kettner worked closely with Franklin D. Roosevelt, then secretary of the navy, to push the location of NTS through government channels.

This photograph shows U.S. Naval Training Station San Diego after the construction of eight additional barracks, a post office, and four officers' quarters along the main road through town known as Rosecrans Street. The inception for the Naval Training Station was predominantly economic. The business elite of San Diego in competition with Los Angeles and San Francisco, both with excellent harbors, had to devise a plan to turn San Diego's marshland into a profit.

The first naval presence in San Diego was a temporary location in Balboa Park. With the onset of World War I and with the encouragement from the city and businesses of San Diego, the U.S. Navy "rented" the home of the recently concluded Panama-California Exposition for its Naval Training Station. In this photograph, the California Tower can be seen in the background with the science and education building, which was torn down in the 1950s.

Recruits in Balboa Park are exercising in front of the Home Economy Building, which was demolished in 1963. They are training for stamina and ship work with rope pulling, sometimes known as the rope game tug-of-war. This and other physical activities were all part of the recruits' training, as it still is today. The goal of military training is to instill and reinforce the navy's core values of honor, courage, and commitment, along with the basic skills of a seamanship in a team environment.

Another sport played for fun was volleyball, which kept the sailors in shape while working in a team environment. Recruits are playing this game in front of the Home Economy Building, demolished in 1963. The U.S. Navy used the Home Economy Building during World War I as a recreation center, complete with pool and billiards tables. When on liberty, the recruits spent time on the Plaza de Panama, where dances and band concerts were held.

Traditionally a sailor at sea must be an expert with ropes and the various techniques for tying and utilizing the rope. Here sailors are fine-tuning their skills in rope tying or knots in Balboa Park. Other training included physical fitness, seamanship, firearms, firefighting, and shipboard damage control, as well as lessons in core values, teamwork, and discipline.

The Navy Band San Diego, shown here, was created while the navy was stationed in Balboa Park, and it continued after the closure of NTC. When it began, there were about 30 to 40 musicians in the band. The band's presence and participation was significant enough during the first stages of the Naval Training Station that two of the four fleet training schools established during the first six months were Bugler and Band School.

Inspection was a regular occurrence for all navy recruits. This inspection is being conducted in Balboa Park, the temporary location for the Naval Training Station. The park commission agreed to lease Balboa Park to the navy for $1 a year during World War I. The camp was capable of training up to 5,000 men at one time for 16 weeks before the recruit was transferred to sea duty.

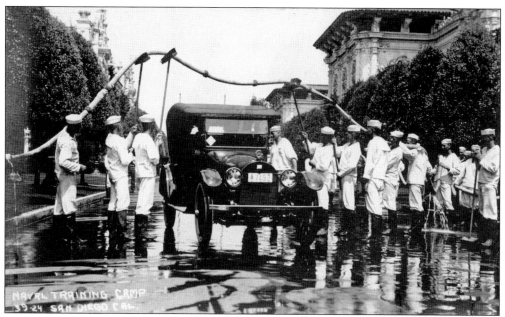

Daily chores are a part of life as a recruit; in this photograph, recruits hold brooms while standing on wet pavement in front of the Casa de Balboa building in Balboa Park. It appears as if the chores have been halted to allow a rather new invention, an automobile, passage. Life for new recruits in the temporary Balboa Park location was rough, as the buildings were not built to house people overnight, especially during the chilly San Diego evenings.

Graduation is something recruits look forward to even more than liberty. In this photograph, graduation is taking place in front of the House of Charm in Balboa Parks exposition ground, now a perfect grinder and graduation ceremonial ground. Capt. Arthur MacArthur most likely is presiding as the first commanding officer of the temporary Balboa Park base. Captain MacArthur was the son of Lt. Gen. Arthur MacArthur, former governor general of the Philippines, and brother of Brig. Gen. Douglas MacArthur, former superintendent of West Point Military Academy.

Inspections were a constant part of recruits' lives. Here inspections are conducted in front of the Science and Education Building in Balboa Park, since demolished. The building had a construction cost of $44,328 and contained an arcade along the south and east side walls with extended overhanging pavilions at the north end. It was one of the most utilized buildings by the navy during their temporary stay.

This view of the parade grounds of Balboa Park shows numerous troops making up the navy flag in front of the House of Charm. The House of Charm was used as the San Diego Museum during the time of the exposition and while the buildings were occupied by the U.S. Navy. The San Diego Museum continued to operate even as the navy trained; the museum association even opened a branch library for the sailors' use where classes in mathematics, hygiene, and medicine were conducted.

A graduation ceremony for a new set of sailors takes place at the temporary Naval Training Station in Balboa Park in front of Spreckels Organ Pavilion, seen in the upper right corner. With 4,500 pipes, it is the world's largest outdoor organ. While the navy leased Balboa Park, they saw no need for the organ and did not maintain the instrument. The space was used instead for lectures and evening movies. The city renovated the organ at great expense after the navy moved to the new facility.

This view shows Balboa Park while in use by the navy during World War I. The temporary training center was not close to the ocean, so the recruits would use the lily pond in front of the Botanical Building as a place for swim training and boat launching. Many aspects of the exposition grounds had to be reused. Since the buildings were temporary structures built for the exposition and not intended to be livable, the recruits hung their hammocks in various places outside rather than in the buildings, which were cold and drafty.

The grounds in front of the House of Hospitality Building make for a perfect marching grinder for the recruits. The grinder is the place the recruit feels like he spends most of boot camp. The navy's goal of marching on the grinder is to transform a civilian into a sailor and an adolescent into an adult trained with all of the skills necessary to perform in the fleet.

This grinder was located in front of the Science and Education Building, where once again recruits are marching and training. The Science and Education Building was demolished to be replaced with a 1960s modern-style building now home to the Timken Museum, which displays the Putnam Foundation Collection of European old masters, American art, and Russian icons.

Part of marching on the grinder includes marching in formation. Grinder formations are taking place in front of the House of Charm. The grinders were sometimes located quite a distance away from the detention camps the new recruit called home. In the temporary NTS in Balboa Park, the new recruits were processed in detention camps located at the site of today's San Diego Zoo and near the Spreckels Organ Pavilion.

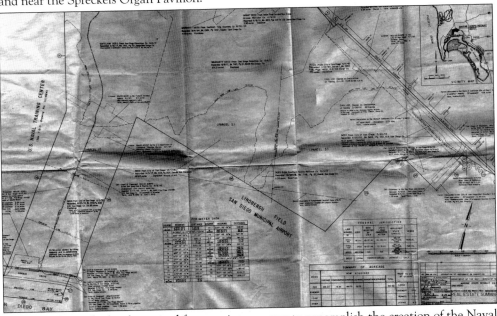

The map shows the land acquired from various sources to accomplish the creation of the Naval Training Station. With the help of Ed Fletcher, funds were raised to acquire the lands from private and corporate landowners to be given to the U.S. government for a Naval Training Station. The chamber of commerce began a campaign to raise $280,000 to purchase 135 acres of land, with John D. Spreckels contributing $10,000 and George Marston, not to be outdone, contributing $15,000. The city council agreed to give the government another 143 acres of marshlands and submerged tidelands.

Once the site was approved, the construction of the new NTS near the town of Point Loma was quick. The infrastructure was built with navy dollars and skills, and the buildings went up with little delay. Ingram Plaza was first the site of the tents or detention camps in the early years of NTS also known as D Camp. This panoramic of D Camp shows how the detention camps were isolated to prevent any possible spread of transferable diseases that may have entered the base. Some of the diseases of concern at the time were chicken pox, measles, polio, and influenza. (NARA.)

This photograph is a detail from the above panoramic of D Camp showing daily duties. (NARA.)

The standard stay for new recruits in D Camp at the new facility at NTS was three weeks. During this time, the navy transformed the young boys into men. The first step to this change was a new haircut and uniform. The 21st-century sailor knows this as "sailorization," described as a program designed to integrate sailors into navy life, shape their expectations for future duty assignments, and give them the tools needed for career and personal success. (NARA.)

The recruits in D Camp lived in tents made of wooden floors and walls and covered with a canvas top. Once D Camp training was completed, the recruit was integrated into the regular boot camp training routines on the base. (NARA.)

The detention camp training was a standard part of boot camp until 1932, when permanent facilities were built for the new recruits. These new barracks facilities were permanent structures with lower and upper floor rooms. (NARA.)

D Camp is visible adjacent to the early Naval Training Station buildings. In 1928, Secretary of the Navy Curtis D. Wilbur visited NTS for recruit graduation. He visited the training barracks schools in John Paul Jones Court and inspected Camp Ingram. A 19-gun salute was fired, and a mass flight of 135 navy planes passed in review over the San Diego Bay in his honor. (NARA.)

This is the Naval Training Center prior to the final buildup of structures in the 1980s. From 1920 through 1940, funds through the Department of Navy and later the Works Progress Act dredged the harbor and built a water system for San Diego that is still in use today. Construction began in 1921, with various phases of renovation and build out occurring over the next 60 years. (NARA.)

Newly graduated young men of Company 18 smile for their class picture. Before graduating, recruits must complete intense Recruit Training Command (RTC) physical training, score well on academic tests, and pass personnel inspections, which included gear, bunk, and locker inspections. Physical fitness tests demonstrated the recruit's ability to work as a firefighter and basic seaman.

Recruits are passing in review as part of their graduation ceremony on Preble Field. Preble Field would witness thousands of graduations where millions of men became active service members. The recruit now a sailor in the U.S. Navy, it was a proud moment for families who watched their boys grow into men and march at graduation.

Two

THE RECRUITS

One of the first steps in the transformation from a civilian to a recruit is the haircut. A recruit sweeps hair clippings from the new recruit's first initiation. Here over 240 new recruits just received haircuts, in total taking less than two hours to complete. The relationship between the recruits, their company commanders, and the demands of the rigorous training, both physical and mental, change the men and women forever. (NARA.)

Gate One is the most remembered gate for many recruits. This was the first gate in NTS and for many years was the only gate kept open at night for sailors returning from leave. The two guard gate buildings flanking either side were always manned. The gate is still located on Lytton Road, and, as part of the historic core, the two guard buildings will continue to flank each side. The decorative steel arch was added in 1932, welcoming all who entered.

Once a recruit graduated from D Camp to the barracks, he was required to keep all of his effects organized and clean. In the barracks building, men slept in hammocks strung up by rope each night. Early barracks surrounded the central open courtyard, also known as the grinder, and housed 100 to 150 men at a time. Often during expansion of the base, the barracks were full, and men would sleep outdoors on the sleeping porches.

Many recruits may remember the dispensary building, as it was available to all recruits for any treatments or pharmaceutical supplies they may have needed. The extreme physical training undergone by a new recruit may have sent him here many times. As the numbers of recruits increased, the need for additional dispensaries was evident, and by the 1930s, there were enough facilities for 52 patients in sick bay. (NARA.)

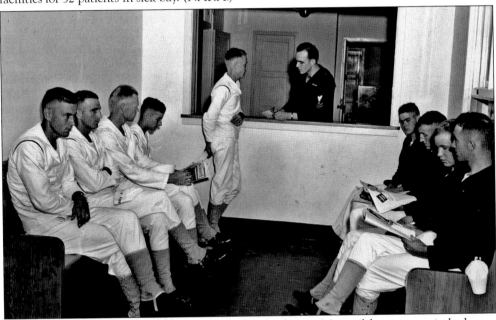

These sailors are waiting for an appointment to see the dentist. Many of the new recruits had never been to a dentist before entering the navy and had to have extensive work done. Without the navy, some may have never had the opportunity to see a dentist or other medical professionals. In the first weeks, recruits went through a battery of medical, dental, and administration screenings, tests, and procedures. (NARA.)

A line of hopeful civilians wait outside Gate One in hopes of joining the navy and training at the Naval Training Station. After the start of World War II, a new influx of recruits began to stream in; the base had to begin a new expansion in order to meet the increasing number of personnel. The new expansion included a new golf course and recreation building.

A caravan overflowing with cheering young men is driving into Gate One. Perhaps these are recruits returning after leave or a group of civilians excited to join up, or perhaps this was the first Christmas at NTS, when Captain Sellers sent eight sailors and a civilian truck driver outside the base to find Christmas trees.

This company of recruits is passing in review, perhaps on the same day Secretary of the Navy Frank Knox visited NTS to review recruit graduation, hand out awards, and have lunch with recruits. On any day, the recruit story is one of personal transformation, experience, and memories, from their arrival on through to graduation day. (NARA.)

This is one of the only early photographs of the interior of the main library at NTS. Boot camp and living in close proximity with others can be difficult for new recruits. The library offered a place sailors could relax, be alone, and catch up on the most recent news events. Having a place for quiet became even more desirable as the population of NTC during the peak of World War II was over 33,000. (NARA.)

The addition of schools was the impetus for the secretary of the navy to change the name from the Naval Training Station (NTS) to the Naval Training Center (NTC) and to add the Service School Command to its list of functions. The change was official in 1944 when NTS became NTC and the three commands were restructured for Recruit Training, Administrative Command, and Service School Command. After a four-week course, some students went on to advanced training. (NARA.)

FIRE STATION —
U. S. NAVAL TRAINING STATION — SAN DIEGO, CALIF.

The first firehouse in the Naval Training Station was located in Sellers Plaza. The firefighting team is smiling while driving the latest in firefighting equipment, the fire engine. All recruits were trained in firefighting, as it is one of the most important phases of training. If a fire breaks out on the ship while at sea, it could have a devastating and deadly result.

In addition to physical training, academic skills, and wartime training, daily chores or duties were an integral part of the sailors' training. Life aboard ship requires everyone to participate in keeping the ship clean and comfortable, and sweeping or swabbing is part of this duty. This photograph shows recruits carrying out a duty every sailor remembers. (NARA.)

Recruits were divided into companies, each consisting of at least 100 men. The companies would very often be pitted against each other to promote teamwork and skill in following orders as well as leadership skills. Competitions included athletic events, and recruits also competed against each other in sea bag and personnel inspections and barracks cleanliness. (NARA.)

In the early years, bayonet exercises were an important part of warfare training. Today the bayonet is used more often ceremonially, as advanced technology, strategies, and warfare equipment have changed. In the beginning, the departments that composed Recruit Training Command (RTC) were Examining and Outfitting Unit, Primary Training Camps, two Advanced Training Camps, Recruit Transfer Unit, Physical Training Division, Rifle Range and Small Arms, Recognition and Lookout Division, Training Aids Division, Fire Fighting Division, Seamanship Division, and four Training Camp Regimental Headquarters. (NARA.)

To be an effective sailor, whether in peacetime or in wartime, one must be physically fit. The strain of maintaining a ship and its crew even during peacetime requires stamina and strength. In this photograph, at what appears to be Camp John Paul Jones, the recruits are led in their physical exercise routines, part of one of their daily activities. (NARA.)

The 12-man rowboat training session is taking place on Pier 445. Built in 1923, this pier had 14 slips and was located adjacent to Preble Field. In 1974, a new sailing marina, Building 549, was constructed with 40 slips and remained NTC's marina until 1989, when it was converted into a club and then in 1996 a coffee shop. After 1989, the new facility, Building 606, eased the increasing demand on the sailing program and the long waiting list for slips. In 1995, during the America's Cup, the name changed to the Navy Sailing Center, Point Loma. (NARA.)

For every new recruit, the task of learning basic seamanship is required. Basic seamanship is where the recruit will learn the basics of line handling, rope tying, and shipboard watch standing, in addition to being out on the water. These three sailors are on a motor launch, a relatively new invention at the time this picture was taken. (NARA.)

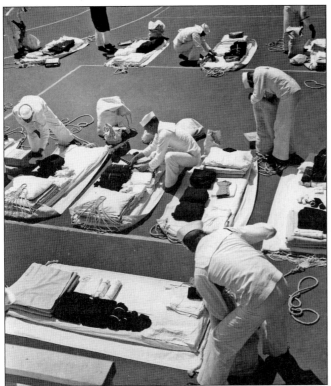

As part of the seamanship training, recruits were required not only to participate but to excel in packing sea bags and in knot tying. Traditional riggings and a variety of knots were used depending on the need—sailors had to be familiar with all of them. In 1934, the NTS received a new rigging loft to train recruits in the art of knot tying. The rigging loft contained a complete set of signals, flags, pennants, and ground tackle. (NARA.)

Gate One was the main entrance into NTC and was always manned. All sailors, whether they manned the gate or not, were required to memorize the chain of command, the general orders, and recognition of rank. Memorizing these standards was especially important for those standing on security watches, as they would often need to challenge people near their post. The need for security was ever increasing, as by 1930, the base had expanded to 235 acres and by 1993 to 550 acres. (NARA.)

Religious services were provided to all recruits from numerous religious faiths and denominations. The North Chapel (the only white building in NTC and today listed as part of the historic core), the Amphitheater (which doubled as a boxing ring or smoker), and later the "Round Church" (located near Bainbridge Court) all offered ceremonies at different times for various religions. A priest, a rabbi, and a Baptist and a Protestant minister were all on-site to conduct services. (NARA.)

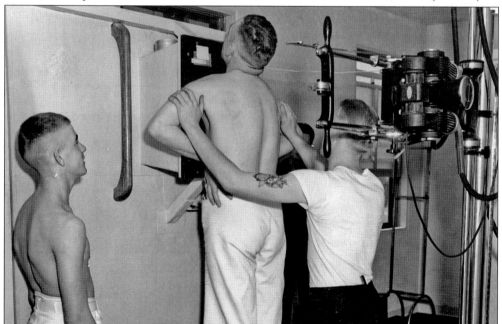

A pharmacist's mate conducts chest X-rays as part of a complete physical on a potential recruit while another waits his turn. For many, an unsatisfactory chest X-ray would mean the end to his navy career. All new recruits had to pass a clean bill of health before entering RTC. Many men discovered medical issues they likely would never have known about until the navy gave them this free screening. (NARA.)

The swimming pool was not only for recreation but also was a key element in the training of the recruit. Many physical exercises and exams were conducted in the pool. A sailor had to know how to stay afloat and stay alive without the use of a personal floatation device in open water long enough to be rescued if he were to fall overboard. A sailor had to know how to remove his dungarees and tie them in a way to catch air so that when placed behind the sailor's head, the dungarees would act like a life preserver. (NARA.)

The Silver Gate Swimmers in 1927 are seen with coach Lt. Benton W. Decker, who coached swimming, along with track, wrestling, and gymnastics, until he left in September. In 1928, a new swimming pool opened that was 60 feet long, 25 feet wide, and 8 feet deep. In 1945, with the need for more room, the Mission Beach swimming pool was used by NTC for recruit training. However, recruits had to march four miles to get there before swimming instruction even began. (NARA.)

Recruit graduation is a daylong ceremony. The event pictured here is a pass in review, the formal military ceremony for honoring the hard work and dedication of the recruit. Many recruits' families are in attendance on graduation day, excited to see their young child, whom they have not seen for months. Many are amazed that they do not even recognize their own child as the transformation is so pronounced. (NARA.)

During the later years of NTC, Recruit Training Command (RTC) was located across the channel and included a ceremonial crossing of the bridge once the initial boot camp was completed. The recruit then moved onto Bainbridge Court, which was located on the western side of the NTC, now the location of the "Homes at Liberty Station." RTC buildings consisted of barracks and the headquarters of the recruit brigade, a mess hall, classrooms, athletic fields, and recreation building. (Rene Cornejo.)

An interior shot shows the barracks in Bainbridge Court during the last year of operation. The recruit barracks included bunks and tables and were where the sailor slept, showered, dressed, and polished his shoes, and where proper folding and stowing techniques were taught. The recruit was responsible for cleaning every square inch of the barracks, which were sometimes called "ships." (Rene Cornejo.)

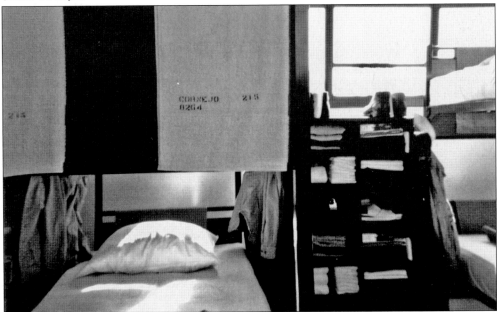

The recruit stored his or her belongings in an open shelf located near the bunks, as seen in this 1993 photograph. For many years, the recruit training maintained the tradition of clothes-rolling, or rolling uniforms in a sea bag, which was then hung near the hammocks. This tradition was later modified: folding clothes replaced rolling, and the recruit began to live out of a barracks locker instead of a sea bag. (Rene Cornejo.)

Rene Cornejo (sitting) and his fellow recruits spend time outside the barracks relaxing during liberty, or time off from the daily routine. Liberty was granted for various reasons and with various potential restriction. Liberty could be short or long; it could be a liberty that allowed the sailor to go off base or a liberty that required the sailor to stay on base. (Rene Cornejo.)

All recruits experience gas instruction during their training. Over the years, the type of gas and the method in which the recruit had to experience it changed. In the 1920s, the navy tested a variety of optical masks on recruits; by the 1930s, molded face masks were tested. The concern at the time was protection of submariners because of the risk of carbon monoxide, chlorine, hydrogen chloride, and sulfur dioxide poisoning. Later gas instruction included training for land and sea, and tear gas was used. By 1990, gas instruction was held indoors and recruits were required to remove their masks for a short period of time before exiting the chamber.

When talking pictures became the rage, the navy was an eager participant. This motion picture enclosure was built in the early 1930s; the theater was actually an open-air facility where recruits could march over in the evenings to watch the latest movies, such as *King Kong* with Fay Wray and *A Tale of Two Cities* with Ronald Coleman. Newsreels were also shown to give recruits weekly updates from around the world. (NARA.)

A favorite recruit pastime for the first 50 to 60 years of NTC history was the smoker, or boxing event. Many recruits would attend these spectacles. This photograph shows the inside of the first boxing arena, built in the late 1920s. The weekly smokers, as they were called, became a tradition throughout the station's history. On the first anniversary of the station, a commemorative smoker was held with more than 2,000 people in attendance. (NARA.)

Every recruit remembers when he joined the navy, where he was, and who he was with. Many new recruits would join together with their friends, and some were fortunate enough to train together. Above, friends Rusty Burkett (left) and Bob Wineberg (right) stand in front of the flagpole at Preble Field. Often high school classmates would find themselves together in RTC, and for many, having someone who came from the same town who understood the adjustment to life in boot camp made the transition easier. The high school classmates from Dubois, Pennsylvania, are also pictured below in front of their new home Barracks 162. (Rusty Burkett.)

The 1960s were a time of renovation and new construction. Renovation began on Building 30, a dormant former galley. The idea was to renovate the galley into a modern cafeteria with a capacity of 400. The renovated space included private rooms and catering services. The navy exchange located in Building 178 was expanded, doubling the store's capacity. The new construction on the Sea Lanes bowling alley is seen on the left. (Rusty Burkett.)

Rusty Burkett is standing outside the new bowling alley under construction. This modern $500,000 bowling alley was located at the south end of Preble Field. The 24-lane bowling alley with state-of-the-art pin setting machines officially opened on July 3, 1965. When it first opened, the entire cost including shoe rental and a game would set you back 45¢. The first manager of Sea Lanes was Earl Petty, who had 26 years of bowling and recreation business experience. (Rusty Burkett.)

On March 5, 1947, Fleet Adm. Chester Nimitz, who was chief of naval operations at the time, presided over the pass in review. Admiral Nimitz was familiar with NTC long before this photograph was taken. In 1931, as a captain, he commanded the USS *Rigel* and decommissioned destroyers at NTC San Diego. (NARA.)

Fleet Adm. Chester Nimitz was an honorary president of the Naval Historical Foundation, was a regent of the University of California, and raised funds to restore the battleship *Mikasa*. His service awards include the Distinguished Service Medal with two gold stars, Army Distinguished Service Medal, Silver Lifesaving Medal, Victory Medal with Escort Clasp, American Defense Service Medal, Asiatic-Pacific Campaign Medal, World War II Victory Medal, and the National Defense Service Medal.

Women first arrived in the navy as WAVES (Women Accepted for Volunteer Emergency Service). Establishing the WAVES required changes in existing legislation, and new legislation had to be written. The law was signed by President Roosevelt on July 30, 1942. Women, just like their male counterparts, had reveille at 5:30 a.m., field days on Fridays, and barracks inspections on Saturdays. They stood duty every four days and had liberty from Saturday at noon until 7:30 a.m. Monday. They took part in sports, including swimming, golf, and bowling. (NARA.)

Women first came to NTC in May 1943 when 15 WAVE yeomen from Stillwater, Oklahoma, reported for duty. By June, 105 women were stationed in San Diego, housed in Sellers Plaza under the guidance of Ensign Vesta Wiley, the WAVE administrator. The women had their own barracks furnished with bunk beds, gear lockers, and bureaus. Many worked in various positions, such as the post office, the base switchboard, and as dental or medical assistants; some were yeomen working for the commanding officer or teletypists in the communications department. (NARA.)

The USS *Recruit* holds, for many recruits, the fondest memories of RTC, as this is where some men experienced their first duty aboard a ship. The USS *Recruit* was designed and built to educate and safely guide young men in the skills needed to maintain and survive aboard a larger and very real ship. Construction of the USS *Recruit* began in 1949 with sheet metal over wood framing on a concrete slab foundation. The sailors in RTC's seamanship division supervised the rigging and used standard navy fittings obtained from salvage ships. Because the USS *Recruit* was moored in a sea of asphalt, it was fondly referred to as the USS *Neversail*. The ship began as a two-thirds scale model of a destroyer escort but was modified once in 1954 for overhaul and repairs, and again in 1982, when based on the training needs of the sailors and newer technologies, the USS *Recruit* was converted into a training guided missile frigate. (NARA.)

Commissioned by Rear Adm. Wilder D. Baker in 1949, the USS *Recruit* is the only officially commissioned non-sailing ship in U.S. naval history to date. Two other training ships were constructed by the navy; however, both have been destroyed, making the USS *Recruit* the last model U.S. training ship in existence. The USS *Recruit* measured 225 feet (69 meters) from bow to stern, with a beam of 24 feet, 4 inches (7 meters) and a height of 41 feet (12 meters) from the tip of the mast to the asphalt. In 1982, the overall length of USS *Recruit* was increased to 233 feet. Over 50,000 new recruits trained annually in basic naval procedure from 1945 to 1989. Among the skills new sailors acquired were correct handling of the marlinespike, ground tackle, cargo boom, deck fittings, signal equipment, and lifeboat, and deck watch as a company of recruits stood watch nightly from 8:00 p.m. to 8:00 a.m. Decommissioned in 1967, the USS *Recruit* was designated as a California State Historic Landmark on August 13, 2005, and is listed on the National Register of Historic Places. (NARA.)

Three

THE SCHOOLS

Recruits are tested during their time at RTC in a number of ways. This 1970s photograph shows the recently graduated recruits taking the test that will determine the next phase of their career in the navy and which training school they will attend. Many new programs and opportunities that began in the 1970s were exclusive to NTC San Diego, including the navy-initiated BOOST (Broadened Opportunities for Officer Selection and Training), which prepared minority sailors for commissioning programs. The BOOST program remained in San Diego until it was moved to Newport, Rhode Island, in 1994 after the closure of NTC San Diego. The navy encouraged opportunities for women long before many corporate and other governmental organizations did. In 1973, Capt. Robin Quigley became the first female commanding officer of the Service School Command, the largest command ever given to a woman officer at that time. (NARA.)

Just as the use of movies became integrated in the training of recruits after the 1937 Buster Keaton film *Tars and Stripes* filmed on location at NTC. This new medium of television was quickly acquired, as the navy could see the benefits to the existing training programs. The new technology required technicians capable of operating the equipment, so the NTC Sound Motion Picture Technicians School was developed. By 1960, this television studio was complete with a closed-circuit television and facilities capable of teaching 2,000 recruits at one time. (NARA.)

The dental clinic at NTC was one of the largest in the U.S. Navy, with six doctors, a chief pharmacist, and a staff of 25. Service School Command quite often would have over 6,000 people in training at one time, so it was essential to provide the recruit basic health needs, since the first 8–12 months were spent in the physically rigorous Recruit Training Command (RTC), or boot camp.

The yeoman class poses for the camera. The first Yeoman A School, for stenography, began in 1944, teaching basics in typewriting, navy correspondence, navy records, reports, forms, shorthand, and stenography. Yeomen are usually assigned duties in an office environment and sometimes work alone with little supervision or work closely with others under close supervision, depending on the assignment. After A School, yeomen are assigned to fleet units and shore stations throughout the world.

Members of the Molder School class of 1957, pictured here, made molds and cores. Their duties included packing in sand and removing patterns after molds had set. The molder may maintain the foundry and operate all types of foundry equipment. The A School course was 16 weeks long and included elementary mathematics, properties of metals, heat-treating, and casting.

Pictured are members of the Molder School class of February 1958. The Service School Command had 21 different schools by 1961; approximately 250 sailors graduated weekly, and the schools ranged in length from 2 to 24 weeks. Following World War II, the center taught fire control systems, sonar, radar, electronic counter measures, and air conditioning to accommodate the technological aviation and maritime advances.

Patternmaker A School, class of 1972, had duties that included making patterns to be used for metal parts such as valves, engine or machine casings, and cylinders. Reading blueprints, roughing out lumber to approximate size and shape, and shaping and smoothing surfaces to exact dimensions were some of their skills. The training was a 16-week course.

Patternmaker A School's class of May 1979 was allowed some changes. During the 1970s, the navy allowed any student scheduled for A School to undergo five days of processing, five weeks of training, and one service week to complete the basic training cycle before their new service school. The remaining recruits had 13 additional days of specialized instruction in the seaman fireman apprentice rating.

The Patternmaker A School class of May 1980 witnessed a huge winter storm in San Diego harbor. Many of the personal and special services boats moored in the marina were in danger of damage. NTC security personnel and Service School Command students assisted the marina, and Pres. Ronald Reagan approved federal disaster aid for California because of damage wrought by the winter storms.

The year 1982 marked the largest BOOST graduation ceremony at NTC: 243 sailors graduated following 10 months of college preparation. The next year, NTC San Diego's RTC provided a 27-man honor guard and navy band performance for England's Queen Elizabeth II. The recruits for this duty were given only five to eight weeks of training. Pictured are graduating members of Patternmaker A School, class of 1982.

Pictured is the Patternmaker A School class of 1986. This year, the Service School Command was the recipient of numerous prestigious awards. As more technical and advanced training were needed, more programs and schools were added to provide post-recruit training. While there were three Recruit Training Centers nationwide, the Service School Command offered unique advanced training available exclusively at NTC San Diego.

Patternmaker A School's class of 1990 witnessed the end of the cold war and a shift in policies and economic superpowers, as the Central Committee of the Soviet Communist Party agreed to give up its monopoly of power and Mikhail Gorbachev was elected as the first executive president of the Soviet Union. In South Africa, Pres. F. W. de Klerk allowed the African National Congress to legally function again and promised to free Nelson Mandela. The United Kingdom and Argentina restored diplomatic relations after eight years.

Here is the Patternmaker A School, class of 1991; NTC San Diego watched this year as defense secretary Dick Cheney recommended closing 31 major and 12 minor U.S. defense facilities and reducing or realigning forces at 28 others. While the Gulf War Operation Desert Storm began air strikes against Iraq, Mikhail Gorbachev resigned as president of the Soviet Union and the Supreme Soviet formally dissolved the Soviet Union.

Patternmaker A School class of 1992 only speculated that the following year would be the final year. NTC was considered for the CNO Bronze Hammer Award for fiscal year 1992. In 1997, the secretary of the navy approved the chief of naval operations' request to disestablish the Patternmaker (PM) and Molder (ML) ratings because of the changing needs and ship force structure within the navy.

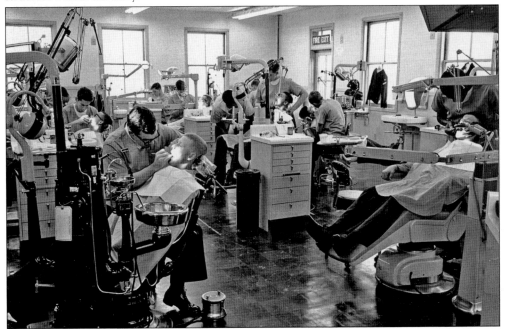

Since the first days of the Naval Training Station, recruits have been required to visit the dentist. Here in 1960, recruits visit during their first week of training. On completion of the first weeks, a commissioning ceremony takes places and each division receives its guidon, the military flag displaying the division number. This ceremony marks the official start of the RTC. (NARA.)

The U.S. Navy (USN) 21-ton Deep Submergence Vehicle Turtle (DSV-3) was located at NTC during sea trials in 1990 These are vehicles capable of deep ocean floor salvage work and retrieval or placement of items. The Turtle, now retired, had a variety of cameras, hydraulic manipulators, and large view ports to operate at depths of 10,000 feet.

This is graduation day for the Radioman A School in 1965. The radio school, called preliminary radio in 1923, changed to Radioman A in 1934. The new school brought new equipment to San Diego, which appealed to recruits, causing Service School Command to see an increase in students wanting to be trained on the latest equipment used during wartime. (Rusty Burkett.)

These recruits are waiting for graduation. In 1961, the school graduated 1,252 students from 25 classes using 124 instructors. The course, the only one of its kind on the West Coast, was 37 weeks of advanced training in maintenance and operations, calculus, teletypes, radio circuits, Morse code electronics, and equipment troubleshooting. (Rusty Burkett.)

The last company to graduate from RTC was Company 215 in the 2,082nd pass in review on November 19, 1993. More than 1,750,000 recruits and 1 million A and C School sailors graduated from the Naval Training Center over the years. (Rene Cornejo.)

Recruit Rene Cornejo is standing with his family on graduation day in 1993 in front of a museum display. In 1986, RTC opened an airman museum in Building 306. Some of the items displayed were an A-7 cockpit replica and models of F-18, F-14, A-7 Corsair, and F-4 Phantoms. Prior to the museum opening, an 18-foot Terrier missile and a 38-foot 19,000-pound Polaris missile were on display in front of the Recruit Training Command headquarters. (Rene Cornejo.)

The mess hall was a place all sailors looked forward to. Operations of the mess hall were handled by the navy cooks, or mess management specialists, who were trained at Service School Command to cook for thousands aboard ship, submarine, or land. After the decommissioning, many items were left behind. These recipe cards were found among those items in the mess halls. This is the cover photograph for the popular recipe "Frankfurters, Cheese and Bacon."

CH-2

Spanish rice was one of the many menu items offered to sailors. San Diego's NTC was the only base with a program for mess management specialist training. In 1958, the secretary of the navy and the International Food Service Executives Association established the Capt. Edward F. Ney Memorial Awards Program. NTC was awarded the Capt. Edward F. Ney Memorial Award, which recognizes the best general messes in the navy. In 1990, NTC San Diego won for food service excellence in the large ashore category.

PINEAPPLE UPSIDE DOWN CAKE   **G. DESSERTS (CAKES, FILLING AND FROSTINGS) No. 29(1)**

Desserts, such as pineapple upside-down cake, were a staple with every meal. The bakery at NTC San Diego was revered by everyone; they were known for their cakes, which were included in almost every celebration and can be seen in many of the official photographs with dignitaries and guest presiding over pass in review. Many graduates moved on to bake at the White House.

PINEAPPLE UPSIDE DOWN CAKE

NOTE: 1. Pans may be greased and lined with paper to facilitate removal of cake.
2. If brown sugar is hard, combine sugar, butter or margarine and 1 cup fruit juice; melt at low heat. Divide mixture evenly between pans; proceed with Step 3.
3. If desired, in Recipe No. G–32, Step 2, 3⅓ cups light fruit syrup or 1⅔ cups heavy or extra heavy fruit syrup combined with 1⅔ cups water may be used. In Recipe No. G–10, Step 1, 7⅛ cups light fruit syrup or 3½ cups heavy or extra heavy syrup combined with 3⅝ cups water may be used.
4. In Step 6, if convection oven is used, bake at 325°F. 25 to 30 minutes or until done, on low fan with open vent.
5. Other pan sizes may be used. See Recipe No. G–G–4.

VARIATIONS

1. PINEAPPLE UPSIDE DOWN CAKE (CAKE MIX): Follow Steps 1 through 3. In Step 4, prepare 7 lb 8 oz (1½–No. 10 cn) Yellow Cake Mix according to instructions on container. See Recipe No. G–G–3, Guidelines for Using Cake Mixes, for more detailed instructions. Follow Steps 5 through 8.
2. PINEAPPLE UPSIDE DOWN CAKE (CRUSHED PINEAPPLE): Omit Step 1. Use 6 lb 13 oz (1-No. 10 cn) canned crushed pineapple. Drain pineapple well. Set aside for use in Step 3. Follow Step 2. In Step 3, omit sliced pineapple and cherries; spread 4¾ cups crushed pineapple evenly over mixture in each pan. Set aside for use in Step 5. Follow Steps 4 through 8.

The recipe for NTC's pineapple upside-down cake is pictured here, the amount of ingredients reflecting the number of people the Mess Management Specialist School was responsible for feeding. The food service division was the third largest in the navy, operating three galleys and supporting BOOST, RTC, Service School Command, and Fleet ASW. In 1990, the three galleys averaged 6,445,000 meals per year.

The smell of bread just coming from the oven is one that many sailors fondly remember. Many recall that early watch aboard ship had its advantages, as sometimes warm bread was available to them before others awoke. This photograph from the 1930s shows the navy bakers at NTC removing loaves of bread from the ovens. In 1940, the base received new equipment for the bakery, including automatic cookie cutters, cake scales, dough mixers, and revolving ovens. (NARA.)

With the new technology in the United States by 1928, the possibilities of flying with rotating blades with the development of a gyroplane became of interest to the navy. By the late 1930s, the Gyro School was established. The gyroplane had four rotating blades and offered a modern fuselage, advanced aerodynamics, and two engines that could produce a speed of 300 horsepower. (NARA.)

Hanging the laundry at NTC San Diego was a duty of every recruit. Other Naval Training Centers upgraded to washing machines and dryers later, but NTC San Diego continued to use concrete scrub tables for washing and laundry lines for drying until the base closed. Recruits were instructed on how to hang their laundry, placing items two fingers apart and turning them in a proper direction while securing them with knots. (NARA.)

Four

The Command

The Command Center, located close to the commanders' homes, overlooked Ingram Plaza and Preble Field. Constructed in 1941, it is the focal point of the base and the location for business transactions and entertaining dignitaries. In addition to offices, conference rooms were available for official meetings. The Command Center is designated historic and is used once again for meetings and special events. (NARA.)

Recruits in RTC stand in review on Ingram Plaza before Admiral Nimitz, who is partially visible on the far right. Behind them is Building 200, the Command Center. These recruits are beginning the transition from civilian to military life while learning the history, tradition, customs, regulations, and basic instruction of naval skills and subjects. (NARA.)

COMMANDING OFFICER'S QUARTER
U.S. NAVAL TRAINING STATION
SAN DIEGO CALIFORNIA

There were four commanders' quarters available for the center command and their immediate family. Stewards would assist running the household. The center command included the admiral command of the center, the station commander in charge of the buildings, the recruit training commander in charge of the recruits, the service school commander in charge of the schools, and the master chief of the command.

The roles of each command were separate yet integrated so as to effectively operate the base. The command master chief was a senior enlisted advisor to the admiral who served as a form of ombudsman for the recruits. The administrative command provided the center's administrative business and human resource services. The Service School command covered over 20 navy schools offering training in the specialized duties, and the recruit training command oversaw the training of the recruits. (NARA.)

Regimental Headquarters - North Unit.

Guards stand duty outside the first headquarters building in Sellers Plaza prior to the construction of Building 200. Additional buildings were added shortly after the commissioning ceremony, including work on the heating system for NTC, a steam heating system that produced rising steam. Recruits remember at various times bursts of warm steam shooting from grates along the sides of the streets like mini geysers. (NARA.)

This view is from the hilltop gardens of the commanders' quarters. The first construction began in 1921, and by 1923 the area known as Sellers Plaza began to take shape. The initial budget was

Station San Diego Calif.

$2 million for the first and second phase. The first contractors, Lange and Bergstrom, constructed Buildings 1 through 13 and later Buildings 14 through 21.

NAVAL TRAINING STATION. SAN DIEGO, CALIF.

In this panoramic view taken years after the previous view, one can see the progression of growth. Behind the camera are the newly constructed commanders' quarters. R. E. Campbell was hired to

construct the Commanders' Quarters A, B, C, and D, as well as Buildings 22 through 24, which were completed with the second phase of the construction.

The view from the commander garden shows NTC's continued growth as contractor Robert E. McKee completed Barracks 25 and 26, the renovation of the southwest wing of Building 1, and

the mess hall, which was designated for use by the new recruits located in the Detention Camp (D Camp).

The streets and drill fields (here shown looking north) were named after naval heroes: the roads from the main gate were Truxton and Decatur Roads, and the cross streets were Roosevelt, Farragut, and Dewey Roads. D Camp became Camp Ingram in honor of Osmond K. Ingram and is now named Ingram Plaza. Camp John Paul Jones, Lawrence Court, Luce Court, and Preble Field were also named after naval heroes. (NARA.)

Large numbers of recruits can be seen in formation in the foreground marching on Preble Field. By 1965, NTC had expanded to include additional camps and the living conditions in the barracks improved with new furniture and a new master gallery with four dining halls. The gallery was located near Bainbridge Court and served 24,000 meals each day to 1,800 people by more than 350 mess cooks.

New Service School Command Barracks 90 and 91, built in 1968, were four-story dormitories accommodating 1,120 students. By the end of the 1960s, more than 20,000 residents lived or worked at NTC. RTC trained more than 50,000 recruits annually, and SSC had 28,000 students enrolled. NTC spent $3,750,000 in San Diego for utilities, contract services, and goods.

Building barracks was only part of the construction. SSC Technical Training Building, Building 94, a three-story, 250,000-square-foot facility located between Truxton Road and Rosecrans Street, had 170 classrooms and no windows to eliminate distractions. This made it possible to teach classified or sensitive material. The building had air-conditioning and closed-circuit televisions in every classroom.

Fleet Adm. Chester William Nimitz, USN, was commander in chief of Pacific Naval Forces for the U.S. and Allied forces during World War II. The inscription on the back of this photograph reads, "To the Commanding Officer, Staff and Recruits of the U.S. Naval Training Center San Diego, California with best wishes—C. W. Nimitz, Fleet Admiral, U.S.N."

The second center commander (after Adm. David Foote Sellers, who served June 1923–August 1926, not pictured) was Rear Adm. Harris L. Laning (September 1926–September 1927). Laning served in the Philippines during the Philippine insurrection and as captain of the U.S. rifle team, which won the gold medal in the 1912 Olympic Games.

Capt. C. W. Cole (September 1927–June 1930) was present throughout the Philippine insurrection, serving aboard both the USS *Baltimore* and the Spanish gunboat *Paraguay*. He served as executive officer on USS *Cincinnati* and USS *Rhode Island*, and during World War I, he commanded USS *Pastores* and the USS *Grant*, and later commanded the USS *Mercy* and USS *Omaha*.

Capt. Sinclair Gannon (June 1930–June 1933) served aboard the USS *Constitution*, USS *Michigan*, USS *Piscataqua*, USS *Kearsarge*, USS *Marchias*, USS *Nevada*, and USS *Connecticut*. In 1912, he was the commanding officer of USS *Elcano*, operating on the Yangtze River during the overthrow of the Manchu Dynasty. In 1918, Gannon was promoted to captain and commanded USS *San Francisco*. He was promoted to rear admiral in 1935 and retired in 1941.

Rear Adm. George F. Neal (June 1933–March 1935) was a lieutenant commander in 1915, commanding the USS *Cummings*, USS *Dorsey*, USS *Ramapo*, and the *Boston*. He was aide to Secretary of the Navy Curtis Wilbur in 1927, and after his time at NTC, Neal commanded the Minecraft Battle Force and served as a senior member of the Board of Inspection and Survey in Long Beach, California.

Capt. David A. Weaver (March 1935–January 1936) went to the Naval War College in Newport, Rhode Island. After completing the course there, he commanded the USS *Eagle*, USS *Quail*, and Submarine Division 17, Pacific Fleet. He came to the Naval Training Station San Diego in 1935 and died at NTC as the commander.

In 1907, Capt. Paul P. Blackburn (April 1936–June 1939). Commissioned captain in 1926, he was the commander of Submarine Division, Asiatic Fleet, in 1928. In 1935, he commanded the USS *California*. After he left NTC, he went to the Naval War College and qualified for command of submarines. In 1944, as his last assignment, he commanded the Northern California sector of the western sea frontier.

Capt. Henry C. Gearing Jr. (July 1940–February 1944) served after Capt. Riley F. McConnell (August 1939–July 1940, not pictured). In 1919, Captain Gearing commanded the destroyer USS *Woolsey*, USS *Somers*, USS *Bruce*, and USS *Maury*. In 1954, he commanded USS *Altair* and was promoted to captain. His awards include the Victory Medal and the American Defense Service Medal. He died during his command at NTC.

Rear Adm. John P. Womble Jr. (January 1948–July 1948) served as commander after Capt. John J. Curley Jr. (February 1944–April 1944) and Commodore R. S. Haggart (April 1944–January 1948). Rear Adm. John Phillip Womble Jr. had World War I service as a midshipman aboard the USS *Ohio*, operating with the Atlantic Fleet. Commissioned an ensign on June 5, 1920, he was assigned to the USS *Mississippi* for one year before being transferred for duty on USS *Mackenzie*. In 1925, he reported to Naval Air Station Pensacola, Florida, for instruction in aviation, and later to Maryland for instruction in chemical warfare at Edgewood Arsenal. He became executive officer of USS *Dobbin* in 1941 and was present on *Dobbin* during the Japanese attack on Pearl Harbor. Promoted to commodore on April 6, 1945, he was instrumental in the first landing of naval forces at Yokosuka, Japan, and was present at the surrender ceremonies aboard USS *Missouri*. In 1954, he was commander of Surface Force, U.S. Atlantic Fleet.

Rear Adm. Frank Monroe Jr. (July 1951–June 1953) served after Capt. E. A. Tarbutton (July 1948–September 1948) and Capt. Joseph A. Connelly (September 1948–June 1951). He served as the officer in charge of RTC in San Diego from 1940 through 1942. In 1949, Monroe was the commanding officer of administrative command, then the assistance center commander, until the retirement of Captain Connolly, when he was promoted to center commander.

In 1953, Capt. Donald F. McLean (July 1953–June 1954) became commanding officer of administrative command, and he was promoted to NTC center commander in five months. During his career, he received the Commendation Ribbon, American Defense Service Medal, Asiatic-Pacific Campaign Medal, World War II Victory Medal, Navy Occupational Service Medal, and China Service Medal.

Capt. Cecil T. Caufield (August 1955–June 1957) served after Rear Adm. Jearne R. Clark (July 1954–August 1955, not pictured). In 1942, Captain Caufield was commanding officer of the USS *Kendrickhe* during the invasion of Sicily. Captain Caufield received the Silver Star Medal and the Commendation Ribbon from the secretary of the navy. He was advanced to the rank of rear admiral on the basis of combat awards.

In 1944, Capt. Ralph Clinton Lynch Jr. (June 1957–June 1959) was awarded the Bronze Star and Commendation Ribbon, the American Defense Service Medal, Fleet Clasp; the American Campaign Medal; Asiatic-Pacific Campaign Medal with engagement stars; World War II Victory Medal; Navy Occupation Service Medal; National Defense Service Medal; and Philippine Liberation Ribbon. He wore the Submarine Combat Insignia.

Capt. Fletcher Hale (September 1964–June 1967) served as center commander after Capt. Oliver Demouy Thomas Lynch (July 1959–June 1960), Capt. Lawrence B. Cook (June 1960–June 1961), Capt. Donald I. Thomas (June 1961–June 1963), and Capt. William Wideman (June 1963–September 1964). Captain Hale attended Western High School in Washington, D.C., while his father was a member of Congress from the state of New Hampshire. In 1933, he entered the Naval Academy and was commissioned an ensign in 1937. Capt. Fletcher Hale received the Silver Star Medal and Bronze Star Medal with two Gold Stars, the American Defense Service Medal, Fleet Clasp, the Asiatic-Pacific Campaign Medal with eight operation stars, European–African–Middle Eastern Campaign Medal, the World War II Victory Medal, the Navy Occupational Service Medal, Asia Clasp, the National Defense Service Medal, and the Philippine Liberation Ribbon with two stars.

Capt. Ralph H. Lockwood (June 1967 to November 1967) was RTC command before becoming center commander. He received three Silver Stars and two Bronze Stars, the American Defense Service Medal (one star), the American Theater Medal (one star), the Asiatic-Pacific Campaign Medal (five stars), the Philippine Defense Theater (one star), the Philippine Liberation Medal (one star), the Victory Medal, World War II, the Navy Occupation Medal, and the National Defense Service Medal (one star).

Rear Adm. Allen A. Bergner (November 1967–October 1969) was awarded the Legion of Merit, Navy and Marine Corps Medal, Bronze Star Medal with Combat V, Navy Commendation Medal, American Defense Service Medal, Fleet Clasp, Asiatic-Pacific Campaign Medal, World War II Victory Medal, National Defense Service Medal with Bronze Star, Korean Service Medal, United Nation Service Medal, Vietnam Service Medal, Philippine Liberation Ribbon, Submarine Combat Insignia with six stars, and the Republic of Vietnam Campaign Medal with Device.

Capt. Harry F. Fischer Jr. (October 1969–June 1970) enlisted in the U.S. Navy as an apprentice seaman in 1935, and while aboard the USS *Ranger*, he took examinations for the U.S. Naval Academy. He entered the Naval Academy in 1936 as a midshipman. After graduating, he was assigned to USS *San Francisco* (CA-38) as a signal officer when the Japanese attacked Pearl Harbor. Fischer was commissioned an ensign in 1960. In 1964, he left for duty as the director of the War Gaming Department at the Naval War College. And in 1968, he became the commanding officer of NTC's Recruit Training Command; by 1969, he had become the center commander of NTC. He retired from naval service at NTC and was presented with the Meritorious Service Medal. Other awards include the Commendation Ribbon with Combat V, the American Defense Service Medal with Bronze Star, the American Campaign Medal, Asiatic-Pacific Campaign Medal with one Silver Star and three Bronze Stars. (eight operations), the World War II Victory Medal, the National Defense Service Medal, the Korean Service Medal, and the United Nations Service Medal.

Before he became center commander, Capt. Arthur T. Emerson Jr. (June 1970–June 1972) was the commanding officer of Recruit Training Command at the Naval Training Center. His decorations include the Bronze Star with Combat V, the Joint Service Commendation Medal, Navy Commendation Medal with Combat V and one Gold Star, Meritorious Service Medal, and the Navy Unit Commendation with one Bronze Star. He also earned the Republic of Vietnam Navy Distinguished Service Medal, American Defense Service Medal with Fleet Clasp, American Campaign Medal, Asiatic-Pacific Campaign Medal with one Silver Star, World War II Victory Medal, Navy Occupation Service Medal with (Asia) clasp, China Service Medal with three Bronze Stars, Vietnam Service Medal with three Bronze Stars, United Nations Service Medal, Philippine Liberation Ribbon, Korean Presidential Unit Citation, and the Republic of Vietnam Campaign Medal with device.

Capt. Ralph Di Cori (June 1972–June 1973) served as the director and antisubmarine tactical training officer at the Fleet Anti-Submarine Warfare School in San Diego. In 1970, Captain Di Cori became the chief of staff at the Naval Training Center, and two years later he served as the center commander. He retired from naval service in 1973. His decorations include the Distinguished Service Medal, Legion of Merit with one Gold Star, Republic of Korea Presidential Unit Citation, American Campaign Medal, American Defense Service Medal, European–African–Middle Eastern Campaign Medal, Asiatic-Pacific Campaign Medal with one Bronze Star, World War II Victory Medal, Navy Occupation Service Medal (Asia), China Service Medal, National Defense Service Medal with one Bronze Star, Korean Service Medal with three Bronze Stars, Vietnam Service Medal, United Nations Service Medal, Philippine Liberation Ribbon, and the Republic of Vietnam Campaign Medal with device.

Capt. Ardwin G. Franch (June 1973–June 1975) served aboard destroyers and cruisers and commanded the tank landing ship USS *Tioga County* and the destroyer USS *Hanson*. He also commanded Destroyer Division 92 and Destroyer Squadron 25. He was the liaison officer for army forces in the Far East and an assistant coordinator for joint chief of staff matters in the Office of Naval Operations. He was promoted to captain while commanding Destroyer Division 92, and while leading task units in North Vietnam shore bombardment operations, he received the Bronze Star. Franch earned a second Bronze Star while commanding DesRon 25 in operations in the Sea of Japan and Gulf of Tonkin. Captain Franch assumed command of the Naval Administrative Command at NTC in February 1972, prior to becoming center commander.

Capt. Homer R. Bivin (June 1975–June 1976) was born in Ventura, California. He joined the U.S. Navy in 1941 and served on the destroyer *Woodworth* in the Aleutian and Solomon Islands campaigns in 1942 and 1943. He graduated the Naval Academy in 1946 and served in the aircraft carriers USS *Boxer* and USS *Coral Sea*. Bivin entered submarine school in 1948, and he served in the submarines USS *Remona*, USS *Bluegill*, and USS *Baya*, all home ported in San Diego. In 1957, he attended graduate school at Stanford University before being assigned to the Bureau of Naval Personnel in Washington, D.C. In November 1970, Bivin was sent to Vietnam, where he served as deputy assistant chief of staff for the Military Assistance Command. He reported to NTC in 1972 as commanding officer of RTC prior to reporting as center commander.

Capt. Thomas J. Porcari (June 1976–June 1978) served as executive officer of the destroyer USS *R. L. Wilson* and the guided missile destroyer USS *Wainwright*. He was an instructor at the Naval War College and the commanding officer of the minesweeper USS *Assurance*, the destroyer USS *Bigelow*, and Destroyer Division 62. During the time he commanded Destroyer Division 62, he also served as assistant chief of staff for operations and as the commanding officer of the destroyer tender USS *Everglades*. He served as assistant chief of staff to the commander on Cruiser-Destroyer flotilla 12, as chief of staff on Carrier Group Six, and commander of Destroyer Squadron 24. Porcari obtained a bachelor's degree in mechanical engineering from Ohio State University and a master's degree in international relations from George Washington University. He was also a graduate of the Naval War College.

Capt. John P. Leahy (June 1978 to December 1979) attended submarine school in 1953 and received a special designator as a submariner, he was promoted to lieutenant junior grade and reported to USS *Volador* as gunnery officer. He obtained the rank of lieutenant commander during his tour with Blueback. Captain Leahy was the executive officer of USS *Bonefish* (SS-582) and then reported to the staff of commander, Submarine Force Pacific, as assistant operations officer. In 1964, he returned to USS *Bonefish* and served as commanding officer until promoted to commander. During his service, he received the Bronze Star with Combat V, a Navy Commendation Medal, a Navy Unit Commendation, a Navy Expeditionary Medal, China Service Medal, Navy Occupation Service Medal, Korean Service Medal, Korean Presidential Unit Citation, United Nations Service Medal, and the Republic of Vietnam Campaign Medal.

Capt. Morris A. Peelle (December 1979–May 1981) was born in Whittier, California, and graduated from UCLA. Commissioned an ensign in 1952, he was designated a naval aviator in 1953. He served as a flight instructor in Pensacola, Florida, and then went to the USS *Ticonderoga*, completing two Western Pacific cruises. Chief of naval materiel, he became commanding officer of RTC prior to becoming center commander.

Capt. Myles E. Fladager (May 1981–September 1981) acted as the navy's liaison with the offices of the secretary of defense, the joint chief of staff, and the state department for foreign policy matters involving Europe and NATO. He was commander of Iceland ASW Group and commander of Fleet Air Keflavik, then reported for duty as commanding officer of Naval Administrative Command, NTC before becoming the center commander.

Rear Adm. Warren E. Aut (September 1981–June 1983) received, among others, the National Defense Service Medal with one Bronze Star in lieu of a second award. His medals and citations for service during the Vietnam conflict include the Republic of Vietnam Meritorious Unit Citation Gallantry Cross Color, the Republic of Vietnam Meritorious Unit Citation Civil Actions Color, and the Republic of Vietnam Campaign Medal with device.

Capt. Herschel L. Plowman (June 1983–October 1984) was commissioned an ensign and designated a naval aviator in 1955; he served as commanding officer of Navy Recruiting District San Diego from 1977 to 1978. He was also commander of Navy Recruiting Area One in Scotia, New York, and responsible for officer and enlisted recruiting in the 10 Northeastern states. Following his tour at Navy Recruiting Area One, he became chief of staff for NTC from 1981 to 1983 before becoming center commander.

Rear Adm. Norman D. Campbell (October 1984–June 1985) was born in Chicora, Pennsylvania, in 1933. He received a bachelor of science degree in education from Slippery Rock University in 1955, enlisted in the U.S. Naval Reserve, and reported for active duty in 1956. His awards include the Legion of Merit, the Distinguished Flying Cross with one Silver Star and one Gold Star in lieu of subsequent awards, the Meritorious Service Medal with one Gold Star in lieu of a second award, the Air Medal with Bronze Numeral 43 and Gold 7, a Navy Commendation Medal with Combat V and four Gold Stars in lieu of subsequent awards, a Navy Unit Commendation, a Meritorious Unit Commendation with one Bronze Star in lieu of a second award, a Navy Expeditionary Medal (Cuba), the American Expeditionary Medal with two Bronze Stars in lieu of subsequent awards, the National Defense Service Medal, the Vietnam Service Medal with two Silver Stars, a Humanitarian Service Medal, the Navy Overseas Service Ribbon, the Republic of Vietnam Meritorious Unit Citation (Gallantry Cross Color), and the Republic of Vietnam Campaign Medal.

Adm. Henry G. Chiles Jr. (July 1985–June 1986) received, among others, the Navy Unit Commendation with one Bronze Star, a Meritorious Unit Commendation awarded to Submarine Squadron 15, a Navy E Ribbon with two Es, a Navy Expeditionary Medal, the National Defense Service Medal, Sea Service Deployment Ribbon, and an Overseas Service Ribbon.

Capt. R. J. Schleicher (June 1986–August 1986), a submariner, took command of SCC in 1982, and in 1985 he assumed duties as chief of staff at NTC and became center commander in 1986. Schleicher's decorations include the Legion of Merit (two awards), Meritorious Service Medal, Navy Commendation Medal (two awards), Meritorious Unit Commendation, the National Defense Service Medal, the Armed Forces Expeditionary Medal, the Vietnam Service Medal, and the SSBN Deterrent Patrol Pin (11 patrols).

Rear Adm. Benjamin T. Hacker (August 1986–May 1988) attended the University of Dayton in Dayton, Ohio, and Wittenberg University in Springfield, Ohio, graduating in 1957 with a bachelor of arts degree in science. He holds the Defense Superior Service Medal, the Legion of Merit, the Meritorious Service Medal, the Navy Unit Commendation, the National Defense Service Medal, and the Armed Forces Expeditionary Medal (Cuba).

Rear Adm. Willis I. Lewis Jr. (May 1988–August 1988) was designated a naval aviator and commissioned an ensign in 1954. He received the Legion of Merit with three Gold Stars in lieu of subsequent awards, the Defense Meritorious Service Medal, the Air Medal with one Gold Star and Numeral 13 in lieu of subsequent awards, the Navy Commendation Medal with Combat V and one Gold Star, the Meritorious Unit Commendation with one Bronze Star, the National Defense Service Medal with one Bronze Star, the Armed Forces Expeditionary Medal (Cuba), the Vietnam Service Medal with one Bronze Star, the Humanitarian Service Medal, the Republic of Vietnam Meritorious Unit Citation (Gallantry Cross Color), and the Republic of Vietnam Campaign Medal.

The decorations of Capt. P. M. Reber (August 1988–July 1990) include the Legion of Merit Meritorious Service Medal with one star, Navy Commendation Medal, Armed Forces Expeditionary Medal with two stars, Naval Unit Commendation with two stars, Meritorious Unit Commendation with three stars, National Defense Service Medal, the Vietnam Service Medal with three stars, the Humanitarian Service Medal Sea Service Ribbon, and the Vietnam Campaign Medal.

Capt. Rodney Knutson (July 1990 to June 1993) received the Silver Star (two awards), the Legion of Merit (three awards), the Distinguished Flying Cross, the Bronze Star (four awards), the Purple Heart (two awards), the Meritorious Service Medal, the Air Medal (six awards), the Navy Commendation Medal (two awards), the Prisoner of War Medal, and various campaign awards.

95

Capt. John C. Ensch (June 1983–June 1995) graduated and was commissioned an ensign in the U.S. Navy in 1965. After completing more than 280 combat missions and being credited with two confirmed MiG-17 kills, Captain Ensch was shot down over North Vietnam by a surface-to-air missile (SAM) in 1972. He was held as a prisoner of war in Hanoi until he returned with the last group of repatriated prisoners in 1973. During his time as a POW, Captain Ensch was tortured and his left thumb amputated by the North Vietnamese. During his career, Captain Ensch accumulated more than 3,000 flight hours and more than 800 carrier landings in F-4 Phantom and F-14 Tomcat fighters. His decorations include the Navy Cross, the Legion of Merit (two awards), Bronze Star with Combat V (two awards), Purple Heart (two awards), Meritorious Service Medal (three awards), Air Medal (18 awards), Navy Commendation Medal with Combat V (three awards), Prisoner of War Medal, Combat Action Ribbon, and various other individual, unit, and service awards.

Capt. Bruce R. Linder (June 1995–October 1995) was awarded a master of science degree in oceanography from the University of Michigan. He holds four navy subspecialty designations, including Anti-Submarine Warfare and Operations Analysis. Some of his awards include the Legion of Merit, the Meritorious Service Medal (three awards), the Navy Commendation Medal (two awards), and the Navy Achievement Medal.

Capt. Stephen L. Drake (October 1995–April 1997 and through the disestablishment of NTC) accumulated more than 4,000 flight hours during his career and 747 arrested landings. His personal awards include the Meritorious Service Medal (two awards), Navy Commendation Medal (four awards), Navy Achievement Medal, and other unit and service awards.

The Sail Ho Golf Course was one of the early features of Sellers Plaza. In 1925, Lt. G. T. Campbell, the first lieutenant of Naval Training Station, was instrumental in the layout of the course, which became a favorite place for recreation and competition. It was also the birthplace of the San Diego's Junior Golf program in 1953 and the Women's Golf Group. Seen here, in no particular order, are Marie Folkers, Jim Borders, Thelma French, and Marigold Gorton.

Women were beginning to have a greater presence at NTC in the 1960s. NTC WAVE Mary Cronin became the first female master chief personnelman. And the Sail Ho Ladies organized. Pictured here from left to right, with one unidentified person, are the master chief officers and committee members of the Sail Ho Ladies: Vi Thomas, Helen Rickert, Karin Murphy, Cleo Rhoades, Irene Howard, Anne Thomas, Mary Jean Anstett, Muriel Anders, Colleen Bennett, Helen Von Christierson, Lu Lieser, and Margaret Ann Koch.

Golf greats such as Phil Mickelson and Craig Stadler played the Sail Ho course. Sam Sneed served as head pro while he trained at NTC. In 1952, two NTC sailors, Gene Littler and Billy Casper, took trophies in the 11th Naval District Golf Championship. Here in 1961, the Sail Ho Golf Course appears very much as it did in 1925. Seen here on the green are Aura Meinert (far left) and Margaret Ann Koch (center).

The 1925 *Hoist* newspaper ran a piece on the Sail Ho Golf Course, stating, "One of the attractive features of the course is the flags marking the holes. The flags have the numbers imposed upon the station insignia, which is a blue diamond trimmed with a red border, in which is centered a white apprentice knot."

Five

THE COMMUNITY

In November 1963, the *Hoist* headlined the news of Pres. John F. Kennedy's assassination. The *Hoist* paper began in 1923 with the opening of NTS and ended in 1993 with its closing. It was one of the navy's oldest continuous internal publications. NTC San Diego had many communities inside the base and outside the base. Point Loma and NTC San Diego shared a relationship economically and socially; the Point Loma community would be invited onto the base during various times over the years, and recruits spent much of their leave visiting Point Loma retailers and establishments. NTC San Diego was also a part of the international community, as it was a frequent host to international visitors during peacetime and wartime. (Vickie S. Bell Cushing.)

In 1990, the Soviets visited NTC admiral Charles R. Larson, commander in chief, U.S. Pacific Fleet, who served as reviewing officer with his Soviet counterpart and guest of honor, Adm. Gennadi Alexandrovich Khvatov, commander of the Soviet Pacific Ocean Fleet. They were joined by Capt. Rodney A. Knutson, commander NTC, and Capt. Robert P. McClendon Jr., commander RTC, in reviewing the recruit graduation.

In the summer of 1990, the 800 Soviet crew members of the three Soviet navy ships—the Soviet Udaloy-class destroyer *Admiral Vinogradov*, the Sovremenny-class destroyer *Boyevoy*, and the Kaliningradneft-class support tanker *Argun*—visited NTC San Diego. Two days before their visit, Belarus declared its sovereignty and independence from the U.S.S.R. Their world was changing while they were away.

The Soviet sailors enjoyed the company of the recruits and the staff while they ate an American dinner at the galley while on a four-day goodwill visit on July 31, 1990, at Naval Training Station, San Diego. It was only two months before their visit that Pres. George H. W. Bush and Soviet Union leader Mikhail Gorbachev signed a treaty to end chemical weapon production and began destroying their respective stocks.

NTC hosted a delegation of Soviet naval officers during the 1990 recruit graduation, and Adm. Gennadi Alexandrovich Khvatov, commander of the Soviet Pacific Ocean Fleet, was the guest of honor. Within a few years, the Soviet navy would cease to be the large force that it had been; many of the destroyers were decommissioned and sold with the breakup of the existing U.S.S.R.

California governor Ronald Reagan was the official guest at the Golden Anniversary Recruit Brigade review. Reagan spoke to the recruits: "I'm sure many of you will continue and this will be your career. . . . This nation has defended freedom in every corner of the world for 200 years with a mixture of career soldiers and seamen. . . . By being in uniform you are doing more to preserve peace than all of those who are preaching their demagogic word from podiums today." Pictured here is Reagan presenting the American Spirit Honor Medal to the top recruit of the graduating company, Constructionman Apprentice Stephan M. Noonan of Company 119.

The Honorable Maureen O'Connor, mayor of San Diego, smiles in front of one of the mess management specialists' famous cakes while participating as a guest of honor in the graduation pass in review. O'Connor was the first female mayor of San Diego and served until 1992. She has been quoted as saying, "I came in as a maverick, and I will go out as a maverick."

Pictured from left to right are Capt. James G. Prout, commander NTC; Pete Rozelle, commissioner for the National Football League; and Capt. Michael Reber, commander NTC, are in the doorway of Building 200 at the Command Center. Pete Rozelle guided the league through expansion from 12 to 28 teams, establishing lucrative television contracts and convincing owners to pool receipts, suspending players for gambling, and maintaining stability during the NFL's merger with the American Football League.

Rear Adm. Richard A. Wilson (left), commander Carrier Group Seven, is pictured with Ralph Gaither (center), a former navy pilot who was a prisoner of war during the Vietnam War for 7 years and 4 months, and Capt. R. A. Knutson (right), center commander. Gaither was promoted to the rank of lieutenant commander during the period he was a prisoner of war, and he became an architectural woodcarver after his return.

Cookie entrepreneur Wally "Famous" Amos (center) poses with Rear Adm. B. T. Hacker (right) and Capt. John P. Kelly (left) after graduation ceremonies. Amos is the guest of honor at the 1990 recruit graduation. Wallace "Wally" Amos Jr. is the founder of the Famous Amos chocolate chip cookie brand and later the cofounder of Uncle Wally's muffins.

Pictured from lef to right, Rear Adm. Archie R. Clemins, commander Training Command U.S. Pacific Fleet, is seen with Carl L. Cobb, retired past command master chief NTC, and Capt. R. A. Knutson, center commander. Admiral Clemins was commander, Pacific Fleet Training Command San Diego, California, and commander, Seventh Fleet, headquartered in Yokosuka, Japan. Admiral Clemins was the 28th commander in chief of the U.S. Pacific Fleet.

Standing in the famous doorway to Building 200, the Command Center, from left to right are Capt. R. O. King, command RTC Great Lakes; Jack Wyatt, district governor of Lions Club International; Brig. Gen. Israel Enav; and the chief of Personnel Management Corps, Israel Defense Corps.

To the Men and Women of the
San Diego Naval Training Center
With best wishes,

Gerald R Ford

Pres. Gerald Ford, the 38th president, visited NTC, the second president to do so since Franklin Roosevelt. President Ford had dinner in the galley along with 900 recruits and gave a speech stating, "I understand that here at NTC you've organized a third party—the marching party. As I'm sure you know, I don't think too much of third parties, so by virtue of the powers vested in me as commander in chief, I hereby order the marching parties for tonight be canceled." Ford then continued by ordering all short tours canceled for the following day. All 900 recruits cheered as President Ford cut the cake, ordering a piece be delivered to every recruit.

Lt. John W. Finn (seen here wearing a hat) congratulates a recruit during graduation ceremonies where he was the reviewing official. Lieutenant Finn, also a recruit from San Diego's NTC in 1926, is a holder of the Congressional Medal of Honor. When Lieutenant Finn was a recruit, he was quoted as saying, "It was real fine military training for infantry drill and manual of arms. Every day we went through what they called the physical drill with arms. You used your rifle as a weight." Finn was born in 1909, enlisting in the navy in 1926. He recalled fondly his recruit days at NTC. He said navy brochures told him navy food was "plain but wholesome." He was surprised when food served in boot camp consisted of roast beef, watermelon, and other fruit. "Definitely the finest navy chow I ever ate," he recalled. Finn became an aviation ordnanceman and worked his way up to chief petty officer in only nine years.

As chief of aviation ordnance, John Finn and his wife, Alice, were stationed in Kaneohe Bay in 1941, the first location attacked by the Japanese prior to Pearl Harbor. As the couple lay in bed on a beautiful Sunday morning, they were roused by the sound of gunfire and airplanes. On the morning of December 7, 1941, when the Japanese attacked, he left his quarters and manned a .50-caliber machine gun mounted in an exposed section of a parking ramp. John Finn spent the next 18 hours, suffering from at least 20 wounds and in need of medical attention, firing on enemy planes and securing the bay; reports indicated he had single-handedly shot down one Japanese aircraft, killing the pilot. "There was shrapnel in my chest and abdomen and I spent 14 days in sick bay," he told the *Hoist*. Nine months later, Adm. Chester Nimitz awarded Finn his Medal of Honor in ceremonies aboard USS *Enterprise*. His citation was signed by Pres. Franklin D. Roosevelt. Finn believes the downing of the plane was the collective action of all the men that morning. (NARA.)

Six

THE LAST REVIEW

This picture, taken by members of Rene Cornejo's family, shows the last pass in review to march onto Preble Field in 1993 as families sit and watch from the bleachers in the background. The Base Realignment and Closure Commission (BRAC) recommended the closing of NTC San Diego, and September 30, 1993, was declared the final date RTC could accept new recruits. (Rene Cornejo.)

The Navy Band San Diego plays for the last time during the 2,082nd and final ceremony to ever occur on Preble Field, where recruits had graduated for 70 years. The last recruits reported to RTC and graduated in a final pass in review on November 19, 1993. Each pass in review ties together the future and history of the navy and naval traditions. (Rene Cornejo.)

This photograph is a view of Preble Field on the final graduation day of NTC San Diego in 1993. It is already beginning to look empty, when once this was a thriving, growing navy community. In December of that year, the Camp Nimitz buildings were the first to close, and the rest soon followed. Fortunately, San Diego mayor Susan Golding formed a task force to recommend a reuse of NTC. (Rene Cornejo.)

The reviewing officer for the final review was Vice Adm. Robert K. U. Kihune, chief of Naval Education and Training. Seaman Apprentice P. J. Walstad Jr. was the recipient of the Navy League Division Honor Recruit Award and outstanding recruit for Company 215 in 1993. During Kihune's career, he commanded the USS *Kitty Hawk*, USS *Nimitz*, and the USS *New Jersey*. Kihune was awarded a Legion of Merit with a Combat V for gallantry. (Rene Cornejo.)

Company 215 was the last company from a group of seven companies comprised of 429 sailors to graduate in the 2,082nd and final ceremony. The official announcement for the disestablishment read, "On March 21, more than 1,000 people will witness the disestablishment of NTC. The ceremony will be held at Ingram Plaza at 2 p.m. where numerous VIPs and dignitaries will be in attendance, including Vice Adm. Patricia Ann Tracey, Chief of Naval Education and Training; the Honorable William Cassidy, Deputy Assistant Secretary of the Navy; Byron Wear, 2nd District San Diego councilmember; and former center commanders." (Rene Cornejo.)

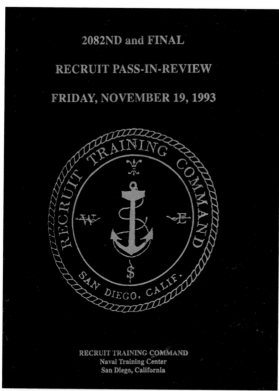

2082ND and FINAL

RECRUIT PASS-IN-REVIEW

FRIDAY, NOVEMBER 19, 1993

RECRUIT TRAINING COMMAND
Naval Training Center
San Diego, California

This is the cover of the official program for the 2082nd and final recruit pass in review on Friday, November 19, 1993. More than 1,750,000 recruits and 1 million A and C School sailors graduated from the Naval Training Center over the years. After the disestablishment, all personnel, equipment, and support were relocated to NTC Great Lakes and other locations consistent with training requirements. (Rene Cornejo.)

The final graduation class picture is a long way from the cover photograph of Company 18, but the accomplishments made by these men are as great as the first graduating class. These are the smiling faces of the last graduating class, closing 70 years of recruit training at NTC. Graduating recruits would now move on to additional specialized training and continue their navy careers as seamen or firefighters, but no longer at NTC. (Rene Cornejo.)

Seven

THE BUILDINGS

NTC had a series of new construction phases throughout its 70 years. This photograph shows the construction of 16 new recruit barracks designed for 3,248 recruits, including a galley with eight different mess halls to accommodate 5,000 people and new medical/dental facilities and headquarters buildings. (NARA.)

It was decided that a new bridge needed to be built across the channel to connect the new Camp Nimitz, which was used for the initial recruit training, similar to D Camp. Because Camp Nimitz was adjacent to Harbor Drive, it allowed recruit companies to march ceremoniously over to the Naval Training Center on completion of their program at the Recruit Training Center. (NARA.)

Construction of the bridge began in early 1952 and cost $70,000. By 1955, the initial phase of Camp Nimitz, which cost roughly $6 million in construction, was complete. Construction began in 1951, when NTC overcrowded with 23,660 sailors and Camp Elliott, built in 1941 as a U.S. Marine Corps training facility and located near Miramar Naval Air Station, was reactivated for NTC's use. This overflow of recruits prompted the NTC to expand. (NARA.)

In this 2008 view, the rooftops of the renovated historic buildings can now be seen in their original 1920 salmon color. Visible are the additional 100 acres of its property, enabling the station to add four more camps: Decatur, Farragut, Luce, and Mahan and a much-needed steam plant to furnish steam heat for the base. An additional 28 acres of land across the channel from Camp Farragut was designated to build Camp Nimitz.

Many of the trees and shrubs planted in 1920 still remain, as seen in this view of Commanders Quarters C. In the 1920s, John G. Morley, who supervised the landscaping in Balboa Park, undertook a landscape project at NTC. A tree committee was formed, and G. A. Davidson, a San Diego citizen, became the chairman. Through the committee, local residents gathered donations of shrubs to beautify the station. Among the first foliage were pistachio trees, century plants, acacias, and palm trees. Within a few years, many of these trees had grown taller than some of the buildings.

In this view, the Corky McMillin Companies Event Center, originally Library Building 177, can be seen renovated and ready to once again be a place of community and a place to gather, in the same way 177 housed the library and offered NTC personnel a place to relax and get away after marches on the grinder.

This is a view looking from the Corky McMillin Companies Event Center toward the newly renovated courtyard. Today NTC San Diego, now Liberty Station, is again a vibrant and uniting place. Residential homes honor the ground of the most recent barracks, and new retail areas occupy the historic commissary, post offices, and restaurants that were once frequented by the NTC recruits. The historic core offers visitors and residents cultural events, dance, and art. The Sail Ho Golf Course is open to all, and historic Sellers Plaza once again greets all who enter its historic gate.

This photograph shows Luce Auditorium awaiting its renovation. Built in 1941 and named for Adm. Stephen Bleecker Luce, it could seat 2,305. Movies for entertainment and lectures for instructional purposes were given here. Not only did NTC produce entertainers, but many celebrities joined NTC to serve during the war, including Humphrey Bogart (World War I); Henry Fonda (World War II); Charles During, the only survivor from his group during D-Day on Omaha Beach; and Douglas Fairbanks Jr. (Navy Reserves in World War II).

This view from the courtyard behind Building 200, the Command Center, is looking toward the new Market Place, renovated meticulously by C. W. Clarke, Inc. Much of the Market Place was originally a marketplace frequented by all recruits, even Hollywood directors William Willie and John Huston, who worked on navy training films. Ernest Borgnine, one of the more famous to come from NTC San Diego, patrolled the Eastern Seaboard for German U-boats during World War II.

Preble Field is seen through the arches of Building 200, the Command Center. Preble Field, once a grinder, was the location of graduation day where many families came to watch their sons graduate as adults. For the recruit, grinders are a painful but memorable part of navy training, as recruits would march for what would seem like endless days.

On the courtyard side of the Command Center, between Truxton and Decatur Roads, is the NTC Foundation's Commemorative Brick program, which allows people to personalize pavers to be placed in one of the Legacy Plazas. It becomes a permanent tribute, honoring the history of the Naval Training Center San Diego and celebrating its future mission for generations.

This 2008 photograph shows the renovated NTC Command Center and the Sybil Stockdale Rose Garden. The rose garden and the Stockdale Tribute at the NTC Command Center were made possible through generous donations to the NTC Foundation from the following: the Vice Admiral James B. Stockdale Board Room, funded by Northrup Grumman Corporation; the Sybil Stockdale Rose Garden in Honor of Navy Families, funded by North Island Credit Union; and the Stockdale Family Exhibit, funded by Supervisor Greg Cox and the County of San Diego.

The renovated Ingram Plaza in 2008 was named in honor of the first American killed in action during World War I, Gunner's Mate 1C Osmond K. Ingram, who received the Congressional Medal of Honor for extraordinary heroism in 1917 during the torpedoing of the USS *Cassin*. Ingram lost his life during this action and was the first enlisted man to have a destroyer named in his honor.

After its closure, the historic portion of NTC San Diego was registered by the National Park Service and is now listed on the National Register of Historic Places. The designation helps preserve the buildings constructed between 1921 through 1949. Forty-nine of the buildings, including the USS *Recruit*, the Ingram Plaza flagpole, the gun platforms on Preble Field, the Sail Ho Golf Course, and several plazas, courts, and landscape elements, are all part of this important designation.

The front of the Command Center is a view many recruits remember, seen here from Preble Field. Once a building for the command offices and a place where important decisions were made, the renovated Command Center is once again active with new conference rooms and events. The buildings of NTC have been brought back to life. At the time of the closure, NTC had expanded to 300 buildings and approximately 3 million square feet on almost 550 acres, including additional training buildings located at Naval Base San Diego on Thirty-second Street.

Ingram Plaza began as D Camp, or Tent City; it later became a grinder and then grounds for smaller ceremonies. Near Ingram Plaza, southeast of Worden and Decatur Roads, the land began underwater and at low tide became a mud flat. NTC undertook a huge hydraulic dredging project to fill in the tidelands, giving NTC 200 more acres for development and creating the two new islands and a channel 600 feet wide.

This newly renovated building was once a sports facility, a restaurant, and an enlisted men's club known as Building 193. The enlisted men's club was the place to be, with a number of dance clubs and a variety of music providing entertainment for everyone. In 1993, the clubs moved to the Blue Jacket Plaza at the Bowling Center complex when the Ship's Bell and famous Glitterdome closed.

The Preble Field guns are now part of the antique collection. Preble Field was named after Edward Preble, born on August 15, 1761, and appointed the first lieutenant in the U.S. Navy in April 1798. He was commissioned a captain in 1799. In 1803, Preble, on the flagship the USS *Constitution*, sailed against the Barbary pirates as commodore of a seven-ship, 1,000-man squadron. Preble's influence extended to the later successes of Stephen Decatur, William Bainbridge, Charles Stewart, Isaac Hull, and David Porter.

This is a view of the historic core of NTC. Landscaping of the area began in 1923 and continued throughout the history of NTC. The first official tree-planting ceremony was conducted at NTC for the first tree planted, a black acacia. The shovel used to plant the black acacia was preserved in a wooden casing along with a plank of wood cut from the tree. The shovel and its casing are part of the antique collections.

The barracks buildings constructed by contractor Robert E. McKee in 1923 are part of the NTC historic core. NTC San Diego remains a proud memory for over a million civilian and military personnel who provided support functions, taught, or received training here.

This is a detail of a balcony in one of the historic barracks. When the barracks were overcrowded, many of the recruits would hang their hammocks outside on these balconies to sleep. The architectural elements are reminiscent of the designs of Bertram Grosvenor Goodhue, the architect for the Panama-California Exposition in Balboa Park. His designs were primarily in the Spanish Revival style, and, as seen in the temporary NTS Balboa Park, an almost Gothic style. Most of NTC San Diego was designed in simpler Mission Revival style.

Our nation's flag, the Stars and Stripes, or "Old Glory," was once again raised over Ingram Plaza on NTC's 84th birthday and in commemoration of Navy Day in 2007. NTC San Diego, Liberty Station, is once again a vibrant community thanks to the respectful renovations of the buildings and grounds and the efforts to maintain the memories of the many men and women who are part of the NTC story. San Diego's Naval Training Center and all of the men and women who called it home will forever be remembered and honored.

ACROSS AMERICA, PEOPLE ARE DISCOVERING SOMETHING WONDERFUL. *THEIR HERITAGE.*

Arcadia Publishing is the leading local history publisher in the United States. With more than 4,000 titles in print and hundreds of new titles released every year, Arcadia has extensive specialized experience chronicling the history of communities and celebrating America's hidden stories, bringing to life the people, places, and events from the past. To discover the history of other communities across the nation, please visit:

www.arcadiapublishing.com

Customized search tools allow you to find regional history books about the town where you grew up, the cities where your friends and family live, the town where your parents met, or even that retirement spot you've been dreaming about.